# HOW TO CARE FOR YOUR NEW HOME

National Association of Home Builders

**How to Care for Your New Home**

BuilderBooks, a Service of the National Association of Home Builders

| | |
|---|---|
| Patricia Potts | Senior Director |
| Design Central | Cover Design |
| Joe Rudden | Composition |
| Gerald M. Howard | Chief Executive Officer |
| John McGeary | SVP, Business Development & Brand Strategy |
| David Jaffe | VP, Construction Liability |
| Marcia Childs | Director, Business Managment Department |

**Disclaimer**
This publication is designed to provide accurate and authoritative information in regards to the subject matter covered. It is sold with the understanding that the publisher is not engaged in rendering legal, accounting, or other professional service. If legal advice or other expert assistance is required, the services of a competent professional should be sought.

— From a Declaration of Principles jointly adopted by a Committee of the American Bar Association and a Committee of Publishers and Associations.

Nothing in this publication should be construed as a warranty (express or implied) or guaranty by the National Association of Home Builders (NAHB) or any persons or organizations involved in the creation of this publication, of any technical descriptions, systems, details, requirements, materials, or products.

NAHB, and the publication's authors and publishers expressly disclaim any responsibility for any damage arising from the use, application, or reliance on the recommendations and information contained herein.



How to Care for Your New Home
ISBN 978-0-86718-804-2

26 25 24 23 1 2 3 4



Cataloging-in-Publication Data available on request.

For further information, please contact:
National Association of Home Builders
1201 15th Street, NW
Washington, DC 20005-2800
BuilderBooks.com

# Acknowledgments

BuilderBooks gratefully acknowledges the thoughtful review of this publication. The work of the Custom Home Builders Committee is greatly appreciated.

**Group Co-Chairs**
Lucy Katz, Katz Builders, Inc.
Austin, TX

Ted Hake, Hake Custom Design
Canton, OH

**Work Group Members**
Wes Carroll, Upright Builders, Inc.
Cary, NC

John Hodgin, John Hodgin Construction Co., Inc.
Greensboro, NC

Justin Kerns, Gary Kerns Homebuilders, LLC, Platte City, MO

Gene Lantrip, Lantrip's Custom Homes, Abilene, TX

Ramie Little, Wellness Within Your Walls, Atlanta, GA

Jerry Passman, Passman Homes, Inc.
Baton Rouge, LA

Phil Warrick, Piedmont Wholesale Engineered Products, Greensboro, NC

Joshua Correa, Divino Homes, Dallas, TX

John Nail, John Nail Homes, Yukon, OK

# Contents

# Welcome to Your New Home

You're getting ready to move into your new home. When you think about it, this is a home that took more than 3,000 components and thousands of people to produce and assemble for you to enjoy.

*How to Care for Your New Home* is a guide to all the different areas of your home, how to maintain and repair these areas. The guide your builder is sharing with you is a resource they have access to because they are a member of the nation's largest and most professional trade association for the residential construction industry, the National Association of Home Builders (NAHB).

As any good guide does, let's start at the beginning – before you move into your new home. Before you move in, the builder does a walk-through inspection of the home with you. During this walk-through, you want to see that everything in the home is what you agreed upon with your builder. Have the builder point out the circuit breaker, water shut-off valve, gas shut-off valve, sewer cleanout, phone box, septic system (if any), and buried tanks and lines (propane, electric, telephone, and cable).

If something is missing or minor repairs are needed, notify the builder onsite and follow up in writing immediately after the walk-through is complete. While telephone calls, conversations, or messages on scraps of paper can get lost or forgotten, documenting all your requests by email creates an electronic trail of the communication between you and the builder.

After you move into your home, there is typically a designated period between you and your builder when you can report any initial issues that come up with the home as you start to live there. If you have any initial issues, make a list of the problems or repair requests and provide it to the builder so they can make the repairs, replace the item or respond to the problem. Circumstances such as adverse weather conditions or temporarily unavailable labor or materials may delay the builder's ability to address the issues, but the builder should work with you to address the problems.

Some of the responsibility for handling some of the service problems fall to the manufacturers and trade contractors who made or installed the various parts and equipment in your house. Start by contacting your builder, who can help explain the information in this guide or direct you to the correct professional who can help.

While the manufacturer, trade contractors, and builder are responsible for creating your home, you are responsible for the day-to-day maintenance of your new home.

This guide helps you understand the role you play in maintaining some of the items in your new home to keep them in working order and keep problems and repair bills to a minimum.

# Get to Know Your New Home

The purpose of this guide is to:

- Introduce the most common components of new homes today
- Provide you with basic information to properly care for and maintain your home
- Prepare you for the minor repairs most new homes require

Some of the items apply to your home and some do not. For example, if you do not have a fireplace, then fireplace maintenance and repair do not apply to your home. On the other hand, your home has some type of heating, ventilation, and air conditioning (HVAC) system and a water supply shutoff valve so every homeowner should be aware of these areas.

The first thing you should do if you have any issues with your home is to contact your builder. The builder can determine if it is a problem covered by warranty. Avoid making any repairs until the builder tells you how to proceed so you do not void the warranty.

## Air-Conditioning Systems (see HVAC Systems)

A properly maintained central air-conditioning system provides years of reliable comfort. Let's look at some of the components of your AC and how you can maximize the life of the system. (See also "Thermostats" under "Heating Systems.")

**Registers & Dampers** — The registers throughout your house help regulate airflow to maintain the desired temperature. By opening and closing the registers and dampers, you can regulate the amount of air that enters a room. Carefully adjusted dampers work with the thermostat to maintain the temperature of your home. If you have a combined heating and cooling system, an HVAC system, the same registers and dampers regulate the flow of hot air to rooms.

In addition to the registers and dampers, which are air outlets, your house has one or more air return registers. It's important to never block any registers or dampers with furniture, drapes, or other objects.

**Filters** — Most central air conditioners have an air filter to help clean the air in your home. You can find the location and how to clean/replace the filter in the instruction manual for the unit.

**Reducing Cooling Costs** — Open doors, windows and fireplace flues, and clogged filters can negate the effects of insulation and cause inadequate cooling (or heating). One way to reduce heating and cooling costs is to close registers and doors to rooms you're not using. For increased energy savings and comfort during the summer, keep windows and doors closed, run heat-generating appliances such as dishwashers or ovens later in the evening, and set your thermostat higher at night. Remember that in the summer, lights, appliances, and people generate heat that makes the cooling system work harder to remove hot air from the home, also increasing cooling costs.

**Annual Inspection** — Your system should be professionally checked and cleaned once or twice a year. See the instruction manual for your system for how often you should have your system professionally serviced.

## Appliances

Whether you have electric or gas appliances, read the instruction manuals and warranty information for each appliance. Fill out and mail warranty documents when you first move into your home. It is helpful to keep a list of authorized service agencies with each instruction manual.

If an electric appliance isn't working, check that it is plugged in and that the circuit breaker is still on. If the appliance still isn't working, then call a repair service to diagnose the problem. (See "Circuit Breakers.")

If a gas appliance with a standing pilot light is not working, check to see if the pilot light is lit. Many gas appliances now use electric ignitions. If you suspect a gas leak, turn off the main gas valve near the meter and immediately call the gas company. **Warning:** Do not light matches, smoke cigarettes, make phone calls, or turn lights on or off in the vicinity of the suspected leak.

## Attics

Attics, or spaces immediately below roofs, vary in size from crawl spaces to areas large enough to be converted into extra rooms.

**Storage** — Storage is one way to use attic space. Some homes are built with roof trusses, which means there is no usable storage space in the attic. If you use your attic for storage, be careful not to put too much weight on your attic floor, which protects delicate insulation and may not be as strong as the floors in the living areas of your home. Attics are susceptible to extremes of heat and cold because attic walls are usually not insulated, so never store combustible or perishable items in an attic.

**Insulation** — Your home has been constructed to be energy code compliant based on the community in which it was built. Do not store anything on the insulation in the attic because compressed insulation is less effective. Occasionally, the insulation on the attic floor may be out of place, which leaves gaps or blocks the path of attic ventilation. Protect your skin, eyes, nose, and mouth, and put the insulation back in its proper place.  Make sure the insulation attached to the access door or pull-down stairs of the attic is secure to prevent heated or cooled air from leaking out of your home.

**Louvers** — Your attic may have louvered openings to allow warm, moist air to escape. Never close or block louvered openings because harmful quantities of moisture may accumulate.

## Bathtubs, Sinks, and Showers

How you care for bathtubs, sinks, and showers depends on the material each is made of. By using proper care, cleaning techniques, and cleaning products bathtubs and sinks retain their luster for many years. However, once damage occurs, the best refinisher in town cannot undo it completely.

Bathtubs, sinks, and showers are made of a variety of materials.

**Vitreous China and Porcelain Enamel** — The surfaces of these fixtures are smooth and glossy like a mirror. While they are durable, they are not indestructible. Carelessness causes chips, scratches, and stains. A blow from a heavy or sharp object can chip the surface, and scraping or banging metal utensils gradually scratches and dulls the surface.

Improper or excessive use of strong abrasive cleansers also dulls and stains shiny new fixtures. Most household cleaners are mildly abrasive but are safe if used with plenty of water. Using a non-abrasive cleaner or baking soda with water is your safest bet.

**Stainless Steel** — Stainless steel fixtures generally resist staining and require an occasional thorough scrubbing. Use a non-abrasive cleaner or a household stainless steel cleaner.

**Plastic and Other Substances** — A non-abrasive cleaner usually works well with plastic and other substances but ask your plumber or the fixture manufacturer for the best way to clean the fixture. For added protection, you can apply a layer of wax or other surface protectors to make cleaning easier and to retain the gloss on the fixture.

**Glass Shower Enclosures or Stalls** — To clean glass shower enclosures, use an ordinary dishwashing detergent (not soap). If there are hard water mineral deposits, use a household glass cleaner. To keep your glass looking clean, the enclosure should be wiped clean after every use. **Warning:** Use ample ventilation, avoid breathing the vapor from the spray, and wear rubber gloves when using glass cleaner.

**Caulking** — When the caulking around your bathtub or sink dries out or cracks, remove the old caulking and replace it. If you don't have a caulking gun, you can buy caulking material in applicator tubes or disposable caulking guns from a home supply store. **REMEMBER:** More is not necessarily better when it comes to caulking. (See also "Drains.")

**Food Stains** — Avoid cutting food on sink drain boards because it can leave scratches and nicks, which makes it susceptible to stains that are hard to remove. To remove most food stains, use a mild solution of chlorine bleach (about 3 tablespoons to a quart of water) and rinse well. For stubborn stains, wait five minutes before rinsing. Do not use chlorine bleach on stainless steel. You can also use a paste of equal parts of cream of tartar, 6 percent hydrogen peroxide, and a household cleaner. Leave the paste on the stain for 10 to 15 minutes before rinsing. (See "Countertops.")

**Mildew** — Even in climate-controlled homes, mildew (another name for mold) can appear in areas of high humidity, such as bathrooms and laundry rooms. You can reduce or eliminate mold growth by reducing the amount of humidity in your home. You can reduce humidity in the home by venting the clothes dryer to the outdoors. Ventilate rooms, particularly kitchens and bathrooms, by opening the windows, using exhaust fans, or running the air-conditioner or a dehumidifier to remove excess moisture in the air. Promptly clean up spills, condensation, and other sources of moisture. Thoroughly dry any wet surfaces or material and do not leave piles of wet towels or clothing in the home.

Regular vacuuming and cleaning also help reduce spore levels. Should mold or mildew develop or grow, scrub clean with a commercial cleaner.

**Paint —** Most oil-based paint comes off easily with paint remover. Newly spilled water-based paint comes off with a cloth dampened in liquid household cleaner. Small paint spots may be removed by scraping with a razor blade. To prevent surface damage, be sure the blade is slanted against the fixture. Remove any residue with a heavy-duty liquid household cleaner and rinse thoroughly.

**Rust Stains —** Rust stains occur on sink or tub surfaces when metal or steel wool gets wet. Rust stains are almost always permanent on fiberglass surfaces.

Ways to prolong the life of bathtubs and sinks:

- Do not let food waste stand in the sink. If you have a garbage disposal, dispose of food waste immediately. If you do not have a disposal, put food waste in a garbage can.
- Do not use bathtubs or sinks to hold paint cans, trash, or tools. When redecorating, cover bathroom fixtures when painting walls, ceilings, and woodwork.
- Do not wear shoes in a bathtub for any reason. Shoe soles carry hundreds of gritty particles that can scratch the surface, regardless of the tub material.
- Do not use photographic or developing solutions in bathtubs or sinks. Developer stains are extremely difficult to remove. (See also "Drains," "Faucets," and "Plumbing.")
- See Drains - Bathtubs, Sinks, Showers, and Toilets for details on how to use a plunger and snake to unclog drains.

## Blinds

Before raising Venetian blinds or opening vertical blinds, be sure that the slats are in the open position. Blinds may be permanently damaged if they are raised or opened when the slats are closed.

**Cleaning —** Dust causes the finish of your blinds to deteriorate. Clean the slats often with a soft cloth or blind-cleaning tool (available in many home-supply stores). Occasionally blinds need to be taken down and washed thoroughly. The tapes and cords should be replaced periodically.

## Cabinets

Avoid using harsh abrasives to clean kitchen and bathroom cabinets (or vanities). Use a detergent solution for laminate wood or metal cabinets. Clean wood cabinets as you would wood furniture unless they are plastic-coated wood cabinets. It is best to ask the builder which cleaners to use on your cabinets. Keep cabinet doors and drawers closed when not in use. Occasionally, check the cabinet hinges and screws to make sure nothing is loose.

## Carbon Monoxide Detectors

Your new home may be equipped with one (or more) carbon monoxide detector. These devices resemble smoke detectors and are designed to sound an alarm if the level of carbon monoxide in the home reaches a harmful point. Carefully review the instructions for the care and maintenance of your carbon monoxide detector. Some units are battery operated and some are wired into the electrical system. Either type should be tested frequently. If the alarm on your carbon monoxide detector sounds, treat the alarm as you would a smoke alarm, evacuate the house immediately, and call the fire department.

## Carpeting (Also see Flooring)

Your carpet should require little maintenance beyond regular vacuuming and occasional cleaning for tough stains or buildup of dirt in high-traffic areas. Most carpeting has built-in stain resistance, which prevents spills and dirt from setting into the fibers. While most stain-resistant treatment is effective, always clean up spills and stains immediately. If you plan to use carpet stain removal products, read the instructions carefully before using. You may want to apply a small amount of cleaner to an out-of-view area of the carpet to test for color fading. Attach furniture rests to the bottom of furniture legs to better distribute the weight of the furniture to help protect the carpet.

## Ceilings (See "Walls and Ceilings.")

## Circuit Breakers

Circuit breakers are the safety valves of your home's electrical system. Circuit breakers protect the electrical wiring and equipment in your home from overloading. Every house should have a master circuit breaker, generally located near the smaller circuit breakers. When the master circuit breaker trips, the electricity to the house cut off. Reset the circuit breaker by switching the breaker off and then back on.

**Electrical Service Entrances** — The electrical service entrance provides power to the service panel and is designed for the electrical needs of the house. Do not tamper with this cable.

**Power Failures** — In case of a complete power failure to your home, determine if it is a neighborhood outage or just your home. Notify the power company of any neighborhood power outages. If the power failure affects only your house, check the master switch and circuit breakers. If one circuit breaker continues to trip, check to see if you have overloaded the circuit. If not, call an electrician. Failure to fix a short circuit can cause a fire. (See "Electrical Receptacles.")

## Condensation

Most houses have exhaust fans in the kitchen, bath, or utility areas that move moist air and odors to the outside. Use these fans when generating excessive moisture, such as when cooking or showering. Turn these fans off as soon as possible because not only do they move moist air outside, but they also move heated or cooled air outside, which can be expensive. (See "Foundations.")

## Countertops

Countertops are generally heat- and stain-resistant under normal use, but they should be protected from hot pots, pans, or baking. Do not cut food directly on the countertop because the knife may dent or nick the surface.

According to countertop manufacturers, most stains wipe off solid surface materials because they are not porous. Stubborn stains can be rubbed off with abrasive household cleaner or fine sandpaper. Countertops made of plastic-coated wood or metal may be cleaned with a detergent solution.

Because marble is easily stained or etched, it should be protected according to the instructions. Compatible sealing, polishing, and cleaning products are available from marble suppliers and some hardware stores.

Granite and solid surface materials do not stain easily and are less prone to scratching than marble. The maintenance of these countertops is minimal, outside of the occasional polishing.

Any countertop or work surface made from unfinished wood requires special care. To protect it from spills, coat the surface (including the edges) lightly with olive or mineral oil, let the oil soak in for a few minutes, and then rub it dry with a soft lint-free cloth. Use several thin coats of oil rather than one heavy coat. To remove onion, garlic, or other odors, rub the surface with a slice of citrus fruit (lemon, orange, etc.), sprinkle lightly with salt, and wipe immediately with a soft cloth or paper towel. Clean with a mild bleach solution once a week. If you do not have a built-in chopping block, buy a portable cutting board to protect your countertops and drainboards.

## Decks

Pressure-treated wood is generally used to build outdoor decks, but decks generally require some maintenance to protect them from moisture. After the moisture from the treatment dries out and periodically thereafter, apply a coat of water repellent and preservative to pressure-treated wood decks. Follow the manufacturer recommendations for cleaning and maintenance of decks made with synthetic or manmade materials. Over time a floorboard may warp, causing a nail to pop up. Screw down or replace the floorboard, if needed. You should have a professional inspection of the deck structure periodically.

## Disposals

If you have a garbage disposal, follow the instructions on how to operate the disposal. Always use cold water when the disposal is on and especially when grinding greasy substances. The garbage disposal cannot dispose of all food waste or grease. Avoid putting fibrous materials such as banana peels or corn husks down your disposal. Also, avoid grinding bones or other hard materials.

Should the drain become clogged, do not pour chemicals down the disposal, especially if you have a septic system because anything you put down the drain can damage the septic system. Check with the disposal manufacturer and your local health department for more information on disposals and septic systems. (See also “Drains” and “Septic Tanks.”)

**Reset Buttons —** Most disposals have a reset button you can push if the disposal becomes overloaded with a substance it cannot grind, which causes the disposal to automatically shut off. If this happens, turn the disposal switch off, remove the substance obstructing the disposal, wait about three minutes, and push the reset button. (See your instruction booklet for the location of the button.) Turn the switch on; if it still does not start, turn it off again and check to see if the circuit breaker tripped.

If the circuit breaker tripped, turn off the circuit breaker (as a safety precaution) and use a mop or broom handle to turn the rotating plate in the disposal until it turns freely. After removing the handle, turn the circuit breaker back on, push the reset button on the disposal, and turn on the disposal switch.

Some disposals come with a special wrench or tool that you can insert into a hole in the bottom of the disposal (under the sink) or the top of the rotating plate. Turn the wrench a couple of times to loosen the material enough so the disposal starts.

**Warning:** Make sure the circuit breaker is off before inserting a broomstick, wrench, or anything else into the disposal.

## Doors

**Sticking** — The most common problem with doors is sticking. If the door is sticking because of swelling, use sandpaper to sand the edge of the sticking door and tighten loose hinge screws. If the door is still out of alignment, sand more or plane the edge of the door. Always paint or varnish sanded or planed areas on the door to protect wood from moisture and help to prevent further problems with the door.

**Warping** — Warping is usually caused by excessive moisture. If a door warps, the best remedy is to dry it in the sun. If the door is still warped after thorough drying, apply weights to the bulged side and leave the weights in place for two or three days.

**Storm Doors** — A storm door may reduce your heating and cooling costs. Storm doors are usually made of aluminum, wood, vinyl-clad wood, or solid vinyl. Houses with insulated steel exterior doors do not need separate storm doors. While less prevalent in mild climates, storm doors can help reduce heating and cooling costs, while also adding a layer of security.

**Weatherstripping** — Weatherstripping is metal, plastic, or rubber that is added to exterior doors to help maintain the energy efficiency of your home. Weatherstripping must remain intact to prevent conditioned air from leaking out of the home and outside air from seeping into the home. If metal weatherstripping becomes loose, bends out away from the edge of the door, or does not seal tightly when the door is closed, re-nail the weatherstripping to see if it resolves the problem.

If it is rubber or plastic weatherstripping, you can re-nail or re-glue with a strong, water-resistant household glue. Do not use a cyanoacrylate (superglue).

**Painting and Cleaning** — Paint wood exterior doors and trim every four to six years. Aluminum, vinyl-clad wood, and solid vinyl doors do not need to be painted. Clean painted doors with a mild detergent. Clean doors with a polyurethane varnish with a damp cloth. Clean doors with other types of varnish as you would clean high-quality furniture. (For care and cleaning of glass in doors, see "Windows.")

**Garage Doors** — Grease the moving parts of garage doors with garage door grease every three months. Tighten the screws that fasten the hardware to a wood door once a year because the wood shrinks a little as it ages, and the screws may loosen.

If a hinged, wooden door sags, tighten or add turnbuckles to bring it back into shape. Each garage door usually requires two turnbuckles, one on each of the two cables crisscrossing the back of the door.

If an overhead door warps inward from being left up for long periods, adjust the nuts on the metal rods or the straps across the top and bottom of the door. Replace bent or cracked panels on wooden doors to prevent other panels in the door from warping or cracking.

Tighten the screws and grease the track and trolley on metal garage doors once a year.

Realign sliding garage doors by tightening the bolts on the wheels that run on the overhead track. Also, check that the floor guide is not out of line.

Leave any type of garage door spring repair to a professional.

**Locks** — You can increase the security of your home by:

- Ensuring locks cannot be reached by breaking a windowpane in the door.
- Making sure a key is available for any inside door locks that require a key to prevent anyone from being trapped inside the house in case of an emergency.
- Attaching chains or locks with screws and bolts that go all the way through the door or frame and cannot be removed from the outside.
- Having a professional install new locks in a metal insulated door. (See also “Security Systems.”)
- Deleting and changing the original and temporary passcode on electronic keyless locks when you move in.

## Drains

Each plumbing fixture in your house has a drain trap, which prevents airborne bacteria and sewer gas from entering the house.

Run water down the sink, shower, and tub drains that are not used regularly to ensure that the drain trap continues to function. Running water through the drains also helps to prevent drying out, bugs, and odors from passing through the trap.

Because of their curved shape, drain traps can easily clog so keep hair and other objects out of drains.

**Bathtubs, Bidets, Sinks, Showers, and Toilets —** If you have a clog, cover any nearby overflow outlet with a piece of old cloth, and if the clog is in a double sink, close the unclogged drain. When the drainpipe from a tub, sink, or shower becomes clogged, try unclogging it with a plunger first. Cover the drain opening with the rubber cup of the plunger so the standing water comes up over the cup edge. Work the plunger up and down rhythmically (rather than sporadically) 10 to 20 times in succession to build up pressure in the pipe.

If the plunger does not work, use a drain snake. You can rent or purchase one at a hardware or plumbing store. Turn the handle of the snake in the same direction when removing it as you did when inserting it to keep snake attachments from coming loose before you remove the snake from the drain.

If the drain can be partly opened with the plunger or snake, pour boiling water (140° F for plastic pipes) down the drain to help unclog it.

If boiling water doesn't work, you can open the trap under the fixture. (The tub or shower trap is usually in a small adjoining closet wall or floor.) Put a bucket or pan under the trap to catch the water and use a piece of wire or plumbing snake to dislodge the blockage.

You can safely use most household drain cleaning products for minor clogs and slow drains, but carefully read the instruction manual.

Treat a clogged toilet as you would a clogged drain. The trap is less accessible so use a steel auger from a hardware or plumbing supply store to unclog the trap. Insert the point of the auger into the trap and turn the handle of the auger to break up or catch the blockage to remove it. An auger is easier to use if one person holds it while another turns the handle. Unclog a bidet the same way as a toilet.

**Prevention —** Add ordinary household cleaning supplies (not baking soda) to drains regularly to help keep them clear of grease. Never pour grease into drains and toilets to prevent clogs. (See also "Plumbing," "Toilets," and "Bathtubs, Sinks, and Showers.")

# Driveways, Walkways, and Steps

Driveways, walkways, and steps are made of concrete, asphalt, brick and other materials.

**Concrete** — Your builder installed contraction and expansion joints as part of your concrete driveways, walkways, and steps to minimize cracking. However, cracking is a common characteristic of concrete. While a method for eliminating cracks is not available, you can make minor repairs to cracks:

- Roughen the edges of the crack.
- Clean out loose material and dirt.
- Soak the old concrete thoroughly so the crack is sopping wet, but not so there is standing water inside the crack.
- Be sure the mixture you buy is appropriate for concrete. Fill the crack with patching cement slightly higher than the crack to allow for shrinkage.
- Cover the patch and keep it damp for several days. The longer the drying time, the stronger the patch.
- When the cement has partly set, remove excess cement with a wire brush. At this stage, the surface of the cement appears sandy.
- Allow the cement to dry and fully set.

**Asphalt** — If you spill oil, gasoline, or similar substances on a black-topped driveway, walkway, or parking area, wash the surface immediately with sudsy water and then rinse. Do not rest sharp objects such as outdoor furniture legs and bicycle stands on the asphalt because they can poke holes in it and never burn leaves or anything else on asphalt.

**Brick** — (See “Exterior Brick Walls” under “Walls and Ceilings.”)

**Winter Safety** — Protect your driveways, walkways, and steps by removing snow and ice promptly. Take care not to gouge paved or brick surfaces while chipping ice. If you cannot remove a stubborn layer of ice, use cat litter, sand, or fine mulch for traction, which are safe for driveways, walkways, steps, and nearby grass or shrubs.

Avoid applying salt in any form. Repeated thaw and freezing with salt and chemicals can damage concrete, brick, mortar, and asphalt and kills grass, shrubs, and trees.

If your driveway has an ice melting system (heated), follow the instruction manual.

## Electrical Receptacles

The electrical wiring in your new home meets the code requirements and safety standards for normal use. Using large appliances or many small appliances on the same circuit can cause an overload. If a circuit breaker trips frequently, contact a licensed electrician to diagnose and correct the problem. (See "Circuit Breakers.")

**Ground-Fault Circuit Interrupters** — The electrical receptacles in your kitchen and bathrooms are equipped with ground-fault circuit interrupters (GFCIs), which are safety devices commonly installed near sources of water to "ground" a person and prevent electrocution if the appliance malfunctions or is dropped into water. GFCIs cut the flow of electricity to the appliance within a fraction of a second if they detect a change in the flow of current to (and from) the appliance. Test your GFCI receptacles monthly by pressing the "test" button.

**Switches** – Your builder may have installed various types of switches such as dimmers and WiFi-enabled. Consult with your builder for more information.

## Exterior Shutters

Keep shutter hinges and mounting brackets oiled and in good condition. Occasionally the shutters will need to be washed thoroughly. Keep in mind that weather elements can cause the finish of your shutters to deteriorate.

## Faucets

Even with normal use, the faucets in your home require occasional maintenance or repair.

**Aerators** — An aerator adds air to the water as it leaves the faucet to eliminate splashing. It also reduces water usage, thereby saving you money. Aerators are most common on kitchen and bathroom sinks.

Cleaning the aerators is the most frequent task in maintaining faucets. To clean an aerator, first, cover the drain. Then, unscrew the aerator from the mouth of the faucet and remove any deposits. Remove and rinse the washers and screens. Replace them in their original order and put the aerator back on the faucet. Water conditions affect how often you should clean the aerators, but generally, every three to four months is adequate.

**Leaks** — All water leaks run up your water bill and leaks can cause water damage to various areas of your home – inside and out. Leaking inside or outside faucets can generally be fixed by replacing the washers. Some faucets with single controls for hot and cold water do not have washers, but their cartridges must be changed periodically. Before attempting to repair a faucet, turn off the water at the nearest intake valve. Washers and cartridges are available at most hardware or plumbing supply stores.

**Outside Faucets** — Drain inside and outside pipes before cold weather begins to prevent the freezing and bursting of outside pipes and fittings. If temperatures fall below freezing in the winter and frost-proof fittings are not provided, turn off outside water spigots. The control valve is usually inside the house close to where the water supply goes through the exterior wall. Remove the garden hose from the spigot and open the outside faucet to drain any excess water.

## Fireplaces

Operate and clean your fireplace and chimney according to the instruction manual and always use caution when using fireplaces.

**Wood-Burning Fireplaces** — Before using your wood-burning fireplace, equip it with andirons (or a grate) and a well-fitted screen, and check to see if it draws properly. To do this, open the damper, light a newspaper on the andirons or grate and see if the smoke is carried up the chimney.

Always open the damper before lighting any fire and keep the damper closed when the fireplace is not in use so warm air does not escape in the winter and cool air does not escape in the summer. Build fires on the andirons or grate — not directly on the fireplace floor. Never burn anything in the fireplace except firewood. Never use kerosene, gasoline, charcoal lighter fluid, or other highly flammable liquids to start a fire, and always be sure the fire is out each night before you go to bed.

Store firewood outside away from the house because it may have insects and hard, seasoned firewood stored outside tends to burn longer. Do not use pine logs in your fireplace because the accumulation of tar can start a chimney fire.

Occasionally, throw a handful of salt on the fire (except in metal fireplaces) to prevent soot accumulation. Have a professional chimney cleaner check and clean your chimney periodically.

**Gas Fireplaces —** A gas fireplace provides the comfort and style of a wood-burning fireplace but requires far less maintenance. Follow the instruction manual for maintenance, safety, and use of your gas fireplace.

Gas fireplaces may have a chimney or may vent exhaust gases (mainly water vapor and carbon dioxide) directly outside without a chimney. If your gas fireplace is vented, the flue or vent should always be open, even when the fireplace is not in use.

Use the same safety precautions with a gas fireplace as you would any gas appliance. Do not smoke while cleaning or lighting the fireplace. If you suspect a gas leak, evacuate the home and call the gas company immediately from a neighbor's house.

**Electric Fireplaces –** If you have an electric fireplace, check the instruction manual before operating the unit. The unit produces a high-temperature heat when in use, so don't touch it and use caution around it.

# Floors

Sub-floors are usually concrete or wood but may be covered by a wide variety of materials to create the floors you walk on in your home. (Also, see "Carpeting.")

Some floors may remain concrete or wood and not be covered with another material.

**Concrete Floors** — Concrete floors are generally maintenance-free but are susceptible to cracking under some conditions. (For repair of such cracks see "Driveways, Walkways, and Steps" and "Foundations.") Occasionally, basement floors collect water from condensation of moisture in the air on cold basement walls. (For treatment of this condition, see "Foundations.")

Apply a concrete sealer to an unpainted concrete floor for easier clean up. Follow the instruction manual for cleaning after the sealer is applied.

Do not clean unpainted concrete floors with soap. Instead, use a solution of 4 to 6 tablespoons of washing soda (sodium carbonate) to a gallon of hot water. (For reference, baking soda is sodium bicarbonate and is a similar compound to washing soda.)

First, wet the floor with water. If necessary, use scouring powder with the washing soda solution to scrub stubborn stains and spills. A stiff brush helps loosen dirt and grime on the floor. Rinse with water.

Clean painted concrete floors with water or a mild soap or detergent solution.

**Hardwood Floors** —Vacuum or dry mop hardwood floors regularly to remove surface dust and dirt. If your floors have a polyurethane finish, vacuum them regularly and wipe them occasionally with a damp (not wet) mop or cloth. Do not use water on hardwood floors finished with anything other than polyurethane. Water sometimes causes the grain to rise, and prolonged use may cause cracks from the expansion and shrinkage of the wood.

Hardwood floors with other finishes need to be waxed periodically with a liquid or paste "spirit" wax. The frequency of cleaning and waxing depends on the amount of traffic. If you use a "self-polishing" liquid wax, be sure it is made for use on hardwood floors.

On moderately soiled floors where traffic is not high, you can use a clean-and-wax product. Before using a clean-and-wax product, remove black marks with dry steel wool and sweep or dry mop to remove loose dirt. Then, apply the clean-and-wax product according to the instruction manual. Rinse the applicator in water to remove any soil.

Clean excessively soiled floors with mineral spirits or household cleaners that leave a protective coat of wax as they clean.

When applying wax or cleaner, keep it away from baseboards to minimize the build-up of wax and extend the life of the baseboards.

Attach furniture rests to the bottom of furniture legs to better distribute the weight of the furniture and protect your floors.

**Engineered Hardwood Floors** – Engineered hardwood floors are hardwood with several layers of laminate on top to add strength to the flooring. In most cases, you clean engineered hardwood floors like a solid hardwood but follow the instruction manual.

**Resilient Floors** — Resilient floors include luxury vinyl tiles (LVT), vinyl, linoleum, asphalt, and rubber. Consult and follow the instruction manual for specific recommendations.

For daily care, remove loose dirt with a broom, dust mop, or vacuum. Wipe up spills immediately, but if a spill or spot dries, remove it with a damp sponge, cloth, or mop. Avoid rubber-backed floor mats because they often yellow vinyl and linoleum flooring.

**Tile Floors** — Clean ceramic tile with a damp cloth or wet mop. For a more thorough cleaning and to remove grime, use a detergent, ceramic tile cleaner, or products recommended by the manufacturer.

Use a stiff brush and mild scouring powder to remove heavy accumulations of film from glazed tile. Scrub or scrape unglazed tile. Clean the joints between tiles with a fiber brush and a mild cleanser. Apply a special sealer for grout to make it more stain-resistant. Always clean spills promptly to avoid staining the grout.

**Cork Floors** — Use a spirit wax or wax cleaner on cork tile. Sand out minor stains with a fine grade sandpaper and re-wax after sanding. Cork floors may need two coats of wax with a buffing after each. Epoxy-coated cork floors are stain-resistant.

**Slate Floors** — Use a sealer on the slate and clean it with a mild detergent solution.

**Marble Floors** — (See care of marble under "Countertops.")

## Foundations

The weight of your house rests upon the foundation, which is the footing — a large mass of concrete poured into a trench — and the foundation walls that rest on the footing. Foundation walls are usually made of poured concrete, masonry block, or wood framing. If you have a basement, the foundation walls also serve as the basement walls. Foundation walls are subject to a wide variety of stresses and strains. Because the base of the wall is in the ground, the basement maintains a relatively consistent temperature. However, the top portion extends out of the ground and may be subject to extreme seasonal temperature changes that can cause concrete and masonry to expand and contract.

**Cracks** — Combinations of stresses and temperature variations may cause cracks in the basement or foundation walls. While these cracks do not affect the strength of the structures, the cracks can be easily repaired, if desired.

To repair medium cracks:

1. Roughen the edge of the crack. (For large cracks, undercut the crack to form a V-shaped groove to a depth about equal to the width of the crack at the surface.)
2. Clean out all loose particles of cement, mortar, or concrete with a wire brush or a thin blade.
3. Wet the crack thoroughly.
4. Be sure the patching mixture is suitable for the job and then fill the crack with patching cement, allowing a little extra for shrinkage.
5. Just before the cement hardens, rub it with burlap or similar material to give it a similar texture to the wall. Wetting a trowel before going over the patch for the last time produces a smooth surface.
6. Paint it to match the rest of the wall, if necessary.

To repair small cracks:

1. Fill the crack with a heavy paste made by mixing dry cement-based paint with a little water.
2. Force the paste into the crack with a stiff bristle brush or putty knife.
3. To match the existing wall finish, use a colored paint to form the paste. Instead of cement-based paint, you can use a mixture of cement and fine sand (one part cement, two parts sand, capable of passing through a 100-mesh screen) mixed with sufficient water to form a heavy paste.
4. For fine or hairline cracks, work cement-based paint into the crack with a short, stiff-bristle brush.

**Condensation** — Condensation takes place wherever warm, moist air inside the house meets a colder surface, such as a window, basement wall, or an exposed pipe. Condensation may look as if moisture is seeping through basement walls or slabs, pipes are leaking, or that water is coming through the windows. A perfectly dry basement can have wet walls because moisture in the air condenses on cold basement walls during the summer months.

Condensation is at its maximum in new homes. When your home was built, gallons of water went into the concrete of your basement walls. This water slowly evaporates, consequently raising the moisture content above normal. Proper ventilation brings this normal drying-out process to its conclusion as steadily as possible. However, do not try to speed up the process by creating extremely high temperatures during the winter, which can cause the house to dry out unevenly and exaggerates the effects of normal shrinkage.

The best way to combat condensation is to close windows during damp, humid weather and open them during clear, dry weather. Providing outside vents for equipment such as a clothes dryer may also reduce condensation. Some warm-air furnaces have humidifiers to bring moisture content in the air up to healthy standards during winter months. If excessive humidity develops, turn the humidifier down or off.

Most houses are equipped with fans in the kitchen, bath, or utility areas to exhaust moist air and odors to the outside. Use exhaust fans when cooking, showering, or generating moist air. Turn exhaust fans off as soon as possible because they exhaust expensive conditioned air to the outside.

**Leaks** — Basement walls are not waterproof but builders damp-proof the underground portions of the foundation to prevent water from seeping in from the soil.

Before making expensive structural repairs to correct wet walls, start by thoroughly checking your drainage system. In many cases, repairing or adjusting downspouts or gutters help to carry surface water away from foundation walls.

If the ground outside your basement slopes toward the wall, build up a "wall" of soil to redirect water drainage away from the house. Avoid planting within 3 feet of the foundation and never water your landscaping toward the foundation. (See also "Landscaping.")

## Gutters and Downspouts

Always keep gutters and downspouts clear of leaves, tree limbs, or debris that could cause overflowing. Point downspouts to direct water away from the foundation and the house. Never paint vinyl gutters but paint is optional for aluminum gutters and gutters made of most other metals. If you do paint gutters, use a rust-retardant paint and re-paint every four to six years.

## Heating and A/C Systems (HVAC)

Heating systems, furnaces, mechanical methods, and installations vary widely by home size and climate. Learn how your system operates, how it functions at maximum efficiency, and what kind of fuel it uses. Never burn anything but the designated fuel in the heating system. If you have any questions after studying the instruction manual for your heating system, your heating contractor can provide answers.

**Thermostats** — The thermostat (usually located on an interior wall) helps to keep your entire house at a comfortable temperature. Individual room temperatures may be further regulated by adjusting the registers in the rooms or the dampers in the ducts from the furnace to the registers. If your home is heated by a forced-air system, your thermostat may also contain controls for the HVAC system.

You can significantly reduce your heating bill by lowering the thermostat during sleeping hours and when your home is unoccupied for a prolonged period. Some homes are equipped with set-back thermostats that can be programmed to reduce the setting before bedtime and increase it before morning. If your home has a heat pump for an HVAC system, do not set back the thermostat unless you are away for a prolonged period.

**Maintenance** — The controls on all types of HVAC systems occasionally malfunction. Such problems are usually solved with a simple adjustment, but unless you are trained to make such adjustments, you should rely on a professional.

Use a professional for annual maintenance and inspection of your mechanical system in late summer or early fall.

**Filters** — Many forced-air systems have air filters that remove dirt and dust from the air. For efficient heating, replace filters at least every three months during the heating season. In some areas, more frequent changing may be necessary. If you cannot see through the filter when it is held up to a light, it needs to be changed.

Usually, replacement involves removing one or two metal screws, pulling out the dirty filter, and inserting a new one, which you can buy from a home supply store. Other systems have latches or dual-stacked filters. Some systems may have electronic air filtering systems. Radiant-type heating systems do not have filters. Read the instruction manual provided by the manufacturer for specific directions.

**Humidifiers** — Some heating systems are equipped with a humidifying device, which requires occasional cleaning to remove accumulated mineral deposits that can interfere with proper functioning. Some systems have an evaporative pad, which may need to be periodically replaced. The instruction manual indicates how often you should do this.

**Pilot Lights** — Some gas furnaces have standing pilot lights for ignition, while most higher efficiency units have pilot-less electronic ignition. If your furnace has a standing pilot light, keep it burning during the summer months. The small amount of heat it generates keeps the furnace dry, prevents corrosion, and readies the furnace for the first cold snap.

**Hot Water Heating System** — With a hot water system, sometimes called a hydronic system, water is heated to about 180° F by an oil or gas-fired boiler distributed through pipes by a small pump called a circulator.

The two most common types of hot water heating systems are radiant and radiant-convection systems. In radiant systems, the hot water pipes may be in the ceiling, walls, floors, or run through baseboard panels on

the outside walls of the rooms. The baseboard heats the wall to about 5 feet above the floor, and the wall itself serves as a radiation panel.

In radiant-convection heating systems, the hot water runs through fine copper pipes behind baseboard panels with openings in the top and bottom to allow the cold air to enter, pass over a set of fins, and rise when it is warmed. Some manufacturers make the two types of heating panels in matching units so they can be interlocked and used together.

**Electric Heating System** — With radiant electric heat, electric heating elements provide the source of radiation. As with hot water pipes, heating elements may be installed in walls, ceilings, and floors, but they are generally found in a decorative baseboard panel.

**Reducing Utility Bills** — The most significant variable affecting your utility bills is your lifestyle. Identical homes on the same street may have utility bills that vary by 100 percent. By living "smarter" in your new home, you can maximize the benefits of insulation and other energy-saving features your builder installed.

Think about the way you live in your home and look for ways to improve the efficiency of your HVAC system. Common sense activities can produce substantial savings:

- Close windows and doors when the HVAC system is on
- Do not run the dryer, stove, or oven on a hot summer day
- Adjust thermostat settings to 68° F (or lower) in the winter and to 75° F (or higher) in the summer
- Open drapes or blinds on the sunny side of the house during winter days to take advantage of natural heat from the sun
- Close the drapes, blinds, or curtains on hot summer days when the sun shines into your home
- During winter vacations, do not shut off the heat so you do not come home to a frozen or burst pipe

## Heat Pumps

Instead of a separate furnace and air conditioner, your home may have a heat pump for winter heating and summer cooling. During the colder months, heat pumps work by drawing on the small amount of heat present in the outside air (or in the ground in the case of ground-source heat pumps) to heat the home. In the summer, heat pumps reverse this process and cool the air in the house by pushing the heat outside of the home.

Most heat pump systems use electric heating elements to supply additional heat when outside temperatures are too low to draw sufficient heat to keep the house warm (typically below about 30° F). Keep utility bills down by setting the thermostat at a constant temperature and by turning off the electric heat source. Avoid manually setting back the thermostat unless you plan to keep the house at a lower temperature for a long period, such as over a weekend or weeklong vacation. Do not use a programmable set-back thermostat with a heat pump.

Follow the instruction manual on changing air filters and other routine maintenance.

## Hoods (See "Ranges, Ovens, and Broilers.")

## Indoor Air

Energy-efficient homes provide maximum comfort at minimum utility costs, but are typically smaller homes with a slower rate of air exchange than older homes. Cigarette smoke, pets, materials used in furniture or carpet, other factors, and products the builder used throughout the home may affect the air quality in your home. Follow the instruction manual and regularly change the air filter in your HVAC system (if you have a forced-air system).

Simple ways to help keep your indoor air healthy are by replacing air filters and regularly letting in fresh air by opening windows and doors. Use kitchen and bathroom exhaust fans to eliminate excessive moisture, grease, odors, and dust, especially when you are cooking or showering. Clean or replace exhaust fan filters as necessary.

# Landscaping

Proper care of the grounds around your home adds to its beauty and protects the structure of the house. A big part of landscaping is how you handle water drainage to keep it away from your home.

**Grading** — Drainage swales or other discharge channels accommodate water runoff and should be kept clear of debris such as leaves, gravel, and trash. Allow 6 inches of clearance between your grading and the wall siding or water may enter the joint between the foundation and the wall material, or the wood may decay. Depressions may form as the soil around the house compacts. Fill any depressions with dirt so that water does not form puddles or cause dampness. Do not block or cover weep holes at grade level or added drainage at your wall system.

**Lawn and Plants** — Water your new lawn and shrubs often but keep the water from hitting the house. In the first fall you're in your home, rake the lawn thoroughly, re-seed it, and add organic fertilizer or manure — giving special attention to bare spots. When watering the lawn, avoid hitting any areas of the house, which can reduce the life expectancy of paint. If you plant anything near the house, always dig the beds several feet away from the foundation.

**The Landscaping Plan** — Not only does a good landscaping plan increase the beauty and value of your home it can also result in lower costs to heat and cool your home over time. Strategically placed trees and shrubs can shade your home in summer and shield it from chilling winds in the winter.

Before you dig a single hole, though, find reliable information about native trees and shrubs for your area. Make a list of plants that appeal to you and consult the Internet for information about them. Once you know what you're going to plant, decide where to plant.

Sketch your property to scale to plot the exact location of the house, walkways, walls, trees, and any other landscape features. Indicate doors and windows too because these can influence the location of plants.

Sketch in the areas you want to reserve for turf and plot each shrub and tree. Try to figure out their space requirements at maturity, particularly if you expect to plant young shrubs or trees. Take care not to plant anything that may grow to block views, shut out natural light, or branches that may grow over your roof.

As you learn about plants, remember that the landscaping around your house is an extension of the indoor living space. The grounds should include defined areas for work and play, often screened or partitioned by trees, shrubs, or other greenery.

Choose plants of various sizes and shapes to attract the eye both near and far. You need taller shrubs for privacy, trees for shade, flowering trees for color, low-growing plants under windows, and thicker evergreens for backgrounds.

The beauty of having a landscape plan is that you don't have to implement the plan all at once. You can work on it a little at a time, as gradually or as rapidly as time and money allow.

## Lighting

Each light fixture may require a certain type of bulb to operate properly. Check each fixture to see the recommended type of bulb.

## Louvers (See "Attics.")

## Motors

The motors of many heavy-duty appliances such as air-conditioners, washing machines, dryers, dishwashers, and others may require periodic servicing. Consult the appliance manual for information about the care of each motor.

## Plumbing

If you have any plumbing issues, address it right away so it doesn't turn into a bigger and more costly problem later.

**Intake Valves —** Become familiar with the water intake valve plumbing system. Label each valve with a luggage tag, in case of an emergency, it's easy to locate the valve you need. Toilet intakes are usually behind toilets, while sink intakes are usually under sinks. The main intake valve is usually near the point where the water enters the house.

**Leaks —** Copper and plastic pipes should last the lifetime of a house, but loose joints need to be re-soldered or repaired by a professional plumber.

If your washing machine, dishwasher, or other water-using appliance is leaking, check to make sure the drain trap is completely open and not clogged. A partially clogged drain can cause an overflow within the appliance. (See also "Drains.")

**Noisy Pipes —** Pipes make noise for a variety of reasons, but the most common reasons are a worn washer, a loose part in a faucet, or steam in a hot water pipe. Fix what is causing the noise because sometimes the noise creates vibration, which can cause fittings to loosen and leak. (See also "Bathtubs, Sinks, and Showers," "Drains," "Faucets," and "Water Heaters.")

**Frozen Pipes —** To prevent pipes from freezing, never leave a house unheated during cold weather. During an extended period of severe cold, provide at least a little heat to unused rooms and baths that are generally not heated. In cold climates, be sure all entrances to crawl spaces are closed during cold weather. For summer homes normally unoccupied in the winter, add RV antifreeze to toilets and drain pipes to protect them. Do not use RV antifreeze in the drinking water distribution pipes.

If a pipe should freeze, first restore heat to the affected part of the house. Open all faucets connected to the lines so that steam can escape if any forms during thawing. Defrost the pipe slowly to prevent steam, which can burst the pipe. Hold a thermometer to the exposed pipe to locate the frozen point and begin to thaw at the frozen point nearest the faucet.

A heat lamp set at least 6 inches from plasterboard or panel-type wall thaws the pipes. In some houses, you can remove the baseboard panel and insert the nozzle of a hair dryer into the baseboard so the warm air blows parallel to the pipes. A hair dryer or heat lamp is also suitable for defrosting exposed pipes.

As the pipe thaws, move the source of heat toward the frozen area until it thaws. If a sink trap is frozen, pour boiling water into it. If a large amount of pipe or an underground pipe is frozen, call a plumber who has electrical equipment for thawing pipes.

## Radon Detectors

Your home may be equipped with a radon reduction system to remove radon gas from the soil under the foundation of your home. Generally, radon reduction systems do not require special maintenance, but be sure to leave the clearly labeled components of this system alone so they function properly.

## Ranges, Ovens, Broilers, and Microwaves

Many ovens and broilers, both built-in and floor models, have self-cleaning cycles or clean continuously. Others must be cleaned by you. Clean the outside of your stove, oven, or broiler with a nonabrasive household cleaner or baking soda sprinkled on a damp cloth or sponge. The manufacturer may make a special appliance cleaner that protects against and cleans stains. If your burner panel or oven front is stainless steel, you may want to use a stainless-steel cleaner on it. Never use harsh, abrasive cleaners on the outside of stoves, ovens, or broilers.

Do not let the oven go too long between cleanings. A lightly soiled oven can be cleaned with a solution of 1⁄4 cup baking soda to 1 quart of water. Rubbing with a paste of baking soda and water may be necessary for some spots. A heavily soiled oven may require a non-corrosive and nontoxic household oven cleaner. Follow directions and cautions closely.

**Electric** — Electric stoves usually have a circuit separate from other kitchen appliances. If your range fails to work, check the proper circuit. (See “Circuit Breakers.”)

**Gas —** If the burners of your stove, oven, or broiler fail to light, check to ensure power is getting to the electric ignition (a clicking sound usually indicates that the unit is functioning). If your stove has a pilot light, make sure that the pilot light is lit. If your electric ignition or pilot light appears to work but the burners still fail to light, there may be a clog, and should be cleaned.

Another cause is the diffusers may not be sitting properly on the burner. If the diffusers are removable, the burners can be soaked clean in a solution of washing soda, but do not soak them in an aluminum pan.

A wire brush or thin stiff wire may be help remove burned food particles from the holes in the gas burners. When using wire, be careful not to push the material too far into the holes. If you suspect that gas is leaking, turn off the main valve (near the meter) and call the gas company immediately. **Warning:** Do not light matches, smoke cigarettes, or use your phone or electrical switches if you suspect a gas leak.

**Hoods —** The filters in range hoods need to be cleaned or changed periodically. For location and directions, consult your instruction manual.

**Microwave Ovens —** Follow the instruction booklet for safety and use. Only use microwave-safe containers to avoid permanent damage to the microwave.

You can remove some spatters and drips from the microwave interior with a damp cloth. Greasy spatters require a sudsy cloth and rinse. A cloth dampened in a solution of baking soda is also safe, but never use a commercial oven cleaner on any part of your microwave oven. Do not use abrasives such as cleaning powders or steel or plastic pads on any part of your microwave oven because it mars the surface.

For exterior cleaning, wipe with a damp cloth and dry thoroughly. Do not use cleaning sprays, large amounts of soap and water, abrasives, or sharp objects on the panel.

## Registers

Floor, ceiling, and air registers should not be blocked in any way.

# Roofs

A properly maintained roof lasts for many years. If a leak occurs, call a qualified roofer to repair it and have a qualified roofer inspect the roof at least every three years. If you go on the roof for any reason, be careful not to damage the surface or the flashings.

Flashing seals are places where the roof meets walls, chimneys, and dormers, or valleys where two roof slopes meet. Be particularly careful when installing a TV or radio antenna because a bad installation can cause serious leaks. To help maintain your roof and gutters/downspouts, keep the roof clean and free of debris.

**Freeze-Thaw Cycles —** Winter storms followed by relatively mild temperatures cause freeze-thaw cycles that can create leaks in roofs.

Most roof shingling is not waterproof but shingles are meant to shed water into gutters or off the roof overhang. Erratic weather conditions can cause a build-up of water—either from snow or ice dams formed on the roof or in gutters and downspouts. This water backs up under the shingles or eventually seeps through the shingles, causing leaks.

Although roofs with a shallow pitch are more susceptible to this phenomenon than steeply pitched roofs, no home is completely immune to the problem. Remove ice from gutters and downspouts, and attempt to remove ice and snow from the lower portions of the roof. In areas of the country where freeze-thaw cycles are prevalent, some homes are equipped with heating elements in their gutters and even part of the way up the roof to counteract the freezing process. (See also "Gutters.")

# Screens (See "Windows.")

# Security Systems

When you move into the home, delete and change the original and temporary passcode for the alarm. Although security systems are installed to work autonomously, you should regularly check that the alarm and circuits are working and inspect sensors one by one. Consult your instruction manual on how to inspect the sensors. Check any primary and backup batteries once a month and replace them at least once a year.

## Septic Tanks

Your builder will tell you if your home is part of the municipal sewer system or if it uses a septic system for waste. With proper care and attention, septic tanks serve as satisfactorily as sewers, but a malfunctioning septic system can become a burdensome expense and a neighborhood health hazard.

If your home uses a septic system, learn the location of the septic tank and its drainage field. For best results, inspect it annually. How often you need to clean out a septic tank depends on its size, daily sewage intake, and the number of people it serves.

Unless the tank is large enough to accommodate additional waste, using a garbage disposal requires more frequent tank cleaning. When the total depth of scum and solids exceeds a third of the liquid depth of the tank, the solids should be removed. With ordinary use and care the tank probably needs cleaning every two years. Your local health department can help you find a service professional.

Because warm weather accelerates bacteria, septic tanks should be cleaned in the spring. The waste material gives off noxious odors and may contain dangerous bacteria so it should be disposed of in a manner approved by your local health department. Chemicals do not reduce solids in a septic tank to the point where cleaning is not necessary.

Consult with your builder, septic installer, or local health department before using any products in your septic system.

## Showers (See "Bathtubs, Sinks, and Showers.")

## Skylights (See "Windows.")

## Smart Home Technology

Your new home may have "Smart Home Technology," such as devices that monitor the water softener, check for water in the basement or update you on a home generator. You may even be able to control appliances like the oven or dishwasher with a smartphone or tablet. Some thermostats, doorbells with video and home security and alert systems use smart technology. All systems need to be set up with the manufacturer guidelines. (Also, see "Door Locks.")

## Smoke Detectors

Carefully review the instruction manual for smoke detectors to familiarize yourself with each unit. Smoke detectors are either battery operated or connected to the home electrical system. Most battery-operated detectors continue to sound until a reset button is pushed. Other types stop automatically when smoke is cleared from the chamber. Check the instruction manual to see what to do if the detector is accidentally triggered. Periodically test the detector to see if it is working properly.

Different types of detectors require different care. Follow the instruction manual for periodic maintenance. Such maintenance may include replacing the light bulbs, replacing the batteries, vacuuming the unit inside and out, and cleaning it with a cotton swab and alcohol. (See also "Carbon Monoxide Detectors" and "Radon Detectors.")

## Steps (See "Driveways, Walks, and Steps.")

## Stoves (See "Ranges, Ovens, and Broilers.")

## Termites

Termites are easier to bar from a new house than to exterminate from an old one. Each spring, conduct your own termite inspection to look for remains of the winged insects. Search the sides of the basement or foundation walls and piers for the earthen tubes that termites build to reach the wood above the foundation. Use the blade of a knife to test wood for soundness. If you suspect the presence of termites, consult a professional exterminator.

## Toilets

Never flush anything down the toilet except toilet paper to avoid stopping up the toilet and sanitary sewer lines. The new low-flush toilets use far less water than previous models and can offer substantial savings on water bills over time. (For unclogging a toilet, see "Drains.")

**Cleaning** — A variety of commercial cleaners are made especially for toilets, but never use them in anything but the toilet. Use according to the directions, but do not mix them or use them with household bleach or any other cleaning product.

**Leaks** — Most toilets have a water chamber, flush valve, overflow pipe, float, and ball valve. If the water chamber appears to leak, the moisture may only be condensation forming on the outside of the tank and dripping to the floor. (See "Condensation" under "Foundations.")

If water leaks into the bowl through the overflow pipe, adjust the float so that it's closer to the bottom of the tank. Flush the toilet, and if it still leaks, the inlet valve washer probably needs to be replaced. If the water trickles into the bowl but is not coming through the overflow pipe, but is coming through the flush ball valve, the connections between the ball valve and the flushing handle may need aligning so the ball drops straight down after the handle is pushed. A worn ball valve or dirt or rust on the ball seat allows water to leak into the bowl. If the ball valve or ball seat is dirty or rusty, clean them. If the ball is worn, replace it.

## Trim and Molding

Trim and molding, such as baseboard quarter-round, may separate from the floor and leave a small gap that catches dust and dirt. This separation is part of the normal process of settling and shrinking.

If the trim comes loose, repositioning and re-nailing it fixes the problem. If a small separation occurs, patch. Use a thin piece of cardboard under the molding to protect the floor when painting the trim or molding.

## Tubs (see "Bathtubs, Sinks, and Showers.")

## Vents (See "Louvers" under "Attics.")

## Walks (See "Driveways, Walks, and Steps.")

## Walls and Ceilings

Your house has two types of walls: bearing and nonbearing. You can alter nonbearing walls without structural damage but altering a bearing wall must be done carefully to avoid reducing its bearing capacity. All exterior walls are bearing walls.

All ceilings are essentially the same in structure but are made of a variety of materials. The structural lumber in your house is the size and grade to safely carry the load. Some shrinkage may occur in these framing members, but your home is designed to settle as evenly as possible.

As with other building materials, wood may contract or expand with weather changes. Heat or cold does not affect it, but it may shrink under extreme dryness or swell under extreme humidity.

**Interior Plaster and Gypsum Wallboard** — Plaster or gypsum wallboards should last for the life of your house. In some cases, normal shrinking in framing boards causes minor cracks and nail pops to appear in wallboard or plaster walls. Popped nails should not affect the strength of the wall and do not require repair.

If you are redecorating a room that has cracks, fill the cracks with spackling compound (available from a paint or home supply store) and a spackling knife. Smooth it out with fine sandpaper and then re-paint or wallpaper the entire surface. Except in very unusual conditions, cracks should not reappear. To prevent cracks wider than half an inch from reopening, apply the spackling compound, then cover the crack with a strip of fiberglass mesh made for this purpose, cover the mesh with thin layers of spackling compound, feather the edges well, and sand smooth.

Unusual abrasions may scuff or indent the surface of plaster or gypsum walls. If this occurs, fill the indentation with two or three applications of joint compound used for taping drywall. Smudges or spots on interior stucco finish may be removed by rubbing it with a fine grade sandpaper (size 00).

**Interior Foundation Walls** — (See "Foundations.")

**Interior Paint and Wallpaper** — Consult your paint and wallpaper dealer for the correct cleaning compound for painted surfaces and wallpaper. If paint starts to blister or peel, there may be an underlying problem. Touch up the spot immediately to prevent it from spreading and look for the cause of the problem, such as moisture penetration through overhead joints or finishes.

**Interior Paneling —** Interior walls may be paneled in wood, cork, and a myriad of synthetic materials, some of which look like wood. Most of these are stain-resistant and easy to clean. Wood paneling may require a special wood cleaner, but some wood for interior walls has been treated or coated so that it is as stain-resistant and as easy to clean as the synthetics. Care of these varies by the material, but most of them can be cleaned with a cloth dampened in a mild solution of detergent and water, followed by a water rinse. Check with the supplier of your paneling to learn what is best for your specific wall surface.

**Exterior Brick Walls —** Brick walls do not contain perfect or evenly spaced bricks. Small surface chips or cracks and slight variations in size and placement are normal and help to create the texture and beauty of brickwork.

The mortar joints in brickwork are subject to weathering over the years. When this occurs, a bricklayer should point the joints up (insert new mortar) to maintain a weather-resistant exterior.

Clean glazed tile or bricks with soap and water. Remove stubborn discolorations by gently scrubbing with a nonabrasive household cleaner or a special tile cleaner.

Use a clay masonry contractor to clean a clay masonry home.

**Efflorescence —** Efflorescence is a white powdery substance composed of one or more crystallized soluble salts that sometimes develop on masonry walls. Scrubbing with water and a stiff brush usually removes it.

**Exterior Wood Siding —** If your home has wood siding, you should not have to worry about wear. Do not overpaint the exterior of your home because excessive painting builds up a thickness of paint that can crack and peel. Scrape, sand, and repaint thin, cracked, or peeling paint on siding to prevent moisture penetration and rot. Coated plywood or plastic-finished wood siding may be guaranteed for the life of the house.

**Aluminum, Steel, Vinyl, Cementitious, and Other Exterior Synthetic Siding —** Many synthetic sidings have a guarantee against cracking, chipping, peeling, and termites for 10 years or more. Most resist marring and scarring and are nearly maintenance-free. Use water and a mild detergent to remove fingerprints around doors and windows. Wash other areas occasionally with a hose.

## Water Heaters

All water heaters have a mechanism to control water temperature, which should be set at 120°F or lower. The lower the temperature setting, the less fuel or electricity used, which could save on your utility bills. Placing an insulation jacket on the water heater can also add savings. Avoid storing anything near the water heater that might obstruct the flow of air or create a fire hazard. For gas heaters, be sure the air intake is not obstructed.

Water heaters normally collect small quantities of scale and dirty water. To remove this material, first shut the water intake valve and turn off the power source for your water heater. Failure to turn off the power source could cause the heating element to burn out.

Then open the valve at the bottom of the heater and completely drain the tank. Open the water intake valve and allow some water to flow through to flush out the remaining sediment. Shut the valve at the bottom of the tank. When the tank is full, follow the instruction manual for restoring heat. In localities with especially hard water, a water softener reduces the cleaning frequency.

**Temperature and Pressure Relief Valve** — This valve prevents a dangerous increase in water temperature and pressure if the thermostat fails. Every three or four months, check the temperature and pressure relief valve on your water heater to be sure the lever works properly.

**Noisy Pipes** — If you hear noises in the pipes when the hot water is on, it may mean that air or steam is in the pipes. The steam may result from the water being too hot. Try reducing the temperature of the water to see if it helps. (See also "Plumbing" and "Faucets.")

## Water Intake Valves (See "Plumbing.")

## Windows

If condensation between the glass panes or broken seals appear, verify your warranty with the manufacturer.

Window frames can be aluminum, steel, wood, solid vinyl, and vinyl-clad wood. Paint wood frames when the house or trim on the house is painted (every 4 to 6 years). Do not paint aluminum, vinyl, and vinyl-clad wood frames. Paint steel frames with rust-inhibiting paint. Allow aluminum to age to a uniform gray because the oxidation (or graying) protects it from the elements. If you prefer to maintain the brighter look, add a coat of wax before it grays. To restore aluminum that has turned gray, polish it with steel wool.

**Skylights** — A skylight or sun tunnel may leak if its seal breaks. Have your seals, caulking, and flashings around skylights inspected for any cracks or interruptions during your roof maintenance inspection.

**Storm Windows** — Dual-glazed windows (two layers of glass with a sealed air space in between) do not require storm windows. In extreme climates, storm windows over insulated glass can save energy and money on heating and cooling the home. When exchanging storm windows during the spring and fall, clean the glass and the screens.

**Cleaning** — Use a piece of crumpled newspaper with a solution of equal parts vinegar and water or 3 tablespoons of denatured alcohol per quart of warm water, or a household glass cleaner to wash the glass. For lightly soiled windows, use a solution of 1 cup of vinegar to 1 gallon of water. Apply the cleaning solution with a sponge or lint-free cloth and dry the glass with a chamois or a dry lint-free cloth. Use a rubber squeegee to speed up the drying process. Clean the window frames with a mild detergent solution. (For marble sills see care of marble under "Countertops.")

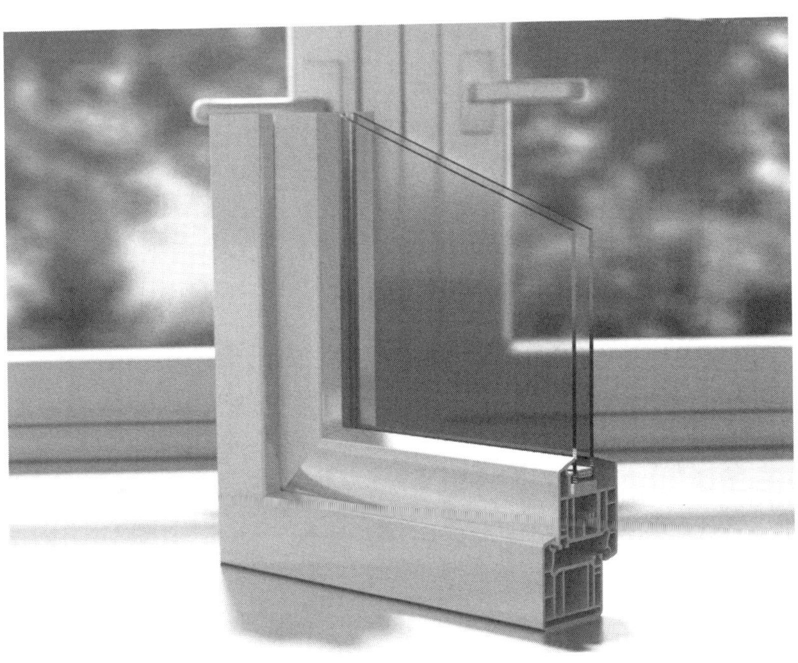

**Minor Repairs** — Wood windows may need new glazing compound occasionally. Remove cracked, loose, or dried-up glazing compound, and clean out dust and dirt with a clean dry brush. Replace any missing glazier points (the small pieces of metal that hold the glass in place). Roll some fresh glazing compound between your hands to stretch it out. Fit it against the glass and the wood with your fingers and smooth it with a putty knife. Mix oil paint with the compound or paint to color it.

For a broken window, remove the remaining glass, all old glazing compound, and glazier points. (**Warning:** Wear gloves!) For a broken window that is not framed in wood, consult a supplier for advice on replacement.

If a window or wooden closet door does not slide easily, rub the channel with a piece of paraffin, a bar of soap, or an old candle. Use a silicone lubricant for metal doors and windows instead of oil because it collects dirt and eventually makes sliding more difficult.

## Miscellaneous Household Tools and Supplies

**Tool Kit** — A few basic tools and supplies help you keep your home in top shape:

- Medium-sized adjustable wrench
- Standard hand pliers
- Needle-nose pliers with wire cutter
- Screwdrivers, small, medium, and large with standard and Phillips heads
- Electric screwdriver
- Claw hammer
- Rubber mallet
- Hand saw
- Assorted nails, brads, screws, nuts, bolts, and washers
- Level
- Plane
- Small electric drill
- Caulking gun
- Putty knife
- Tape measure

Other tools can be rented or purchased as needed.

**Fire Extinguisher** — Buy and store at least one multipurpose fire extinguisher in your home. Make sure every member of the household knows where the fire extinguisher is and how to use it. Check it annually to make sure it is fully charged and functions properly.

Also, make sure that every member of the household knows how to turn off the electricity, gas, and water in the event of an emergency.

**First Aid Kit** — Keep a home first aid kit or supplies with a booklet on first aid in a convenient location.

**Duplicate Keys** — Make copies of the original door keys and keep the copies in convenient places. When you go on vacation, leave a key with a trusted neighbor in case of an emergency.

# Annual Checklist*

- ❑ Check the condition of glazing compound, caulking, and exterior paint. Replace or paint as needed (spring).
- ❑ Exchange glass and screens in storm doors and windows (autumn and spring).
- ❑ Inspect the roof for snow damage; repair it if necessary (spring).
- ❑ Check for evidence of termites (spring).
- ❑ Check interior paint and redecorate when necessary.
- ❑ Seed and feed the lawn (spring and/or autumn); plant annuals (spring); do appropriate pruning of perennials (some in spring, others in summer or autumn); rake and compost leaves; mulch perennials that need winter protection.
- ❑ Remove hose connections and store hose to avoid freezing (autumn).
- ❑ Keep driveways, walkways, and steps free of ice and snow to avoid damage to them and to prevent hazardous walking and driving conditions.
- ❑ Have your HVAC system checked, cleaned and repaired, if necessary. If your unit has an air filter, replace it at least every 3 months during each heating season.
- ❑ If you have a separate air-conditioning system, clean and change filters as the manufacturer recommends.
- ❑ Oil appliance motors as directed in instruction manuals.
- ❑ Check cords and plugs of all electrical appliances for wear. If necessary, have them repaired or replaced.
- ❑ Test your smoke detectors, carbon monoxide detector, and radon detector for proper operation. Be sure to clean the unit (with a vacuum or swab), clean the filter (if any), and replace batteries and light bulbs when necessary.
- ❑ For security systems, check that the alarm and circuits are in working order; inspect the sensors one by one; and check primary and backup batteries once a month.
- ❑ Inspect that all doors and windows operate and close properly.

- ❑ Clean all window tracks, clean and adjust the door thresholds, and check the weatherstripping on windows and doors.
- ❑ Check the attic insulation to be sure the entire ceiling area is covered. Check the eaves to be sure the insulation is not blocking the vents. Make sure insulation is not touching the underside of the roof sheathing.
- ❑ Clean weep holes on all window and door sliders. Dry lubricate all window tracks to make opening and shutting windows easier.
- ❑ Make a careful safety inspection of your home, inside and out, to seek out problem areas.
- ❑ Check for and dispose of fire hazards such as oily rags, unvented gas cans, painting supplies, or flammable cleaning materials in storage areas, backs of closets, basement corners, etc.
- ❑ Check stairs, steps, and ladders for broken or hazardous areas that could cause an accident. Check handrails and railings for sturdiness and reliability.
- ❑ Test all the lights to be sure they work.
- ❑ Check all connections to your electrical system to correct any possible hazards. Replace frayed electrical cords and do not overload extension cords.

Make a detailed checklist of all inspections and repairs required in your home. Leave spaces so that you can record the items as completed. An example of such a list is on pages 45-54 of this booklet. **Visit https://www.nahb.org/other/builderbooks/how-to-care-for-your-new-home** for an electronic copy.

* Some of the items on the annual checklist do not apply to your home.

# Owner's Maintenance Record

| Interior | Dates Checked | | | Remarks |
|---|---|---|---|---|
| **Appliances** | | | | |
| Ranges, ovens, broilers—controls, thermostats, timers, surfaces, heating elements, pilots, and valves | | | | |
| Electrical cords and plugs | | | | |
| Smoke/Carbon/Radon detectors | | | | |
| Security systems | | | | |
| Fire extinguisher | | | | |
| Washer and dryer — vents and connections | | | | |
| **Attic** | | | | |
| Louvers and vents | | | | |
| Insulation | | | | |
| Inside roof sheathing | | | | |
| Electrical wiring | | | | |
| **Basement** | | | | |
| Masonry joints and surfaces | | | | |
| Flooring | | | | |
| Stairs | | | | |
| Insulation | | | | |

| Interior | Dates Checked | | | Remarks |
|---|---|---|---|---|
| **Baths, Sinks, and Showers (see "Plumbing")** | | | | |
| Surfaces | | | | |
| Caulking | | | | |
| Grouting | | | | |
| **Electrical** | | | | |
| Service entrance | | | | |
| Circuit breakers | | | | |
| Outlets and switches | | | | |
| Fixtures | | | | |
| Light bulbs | | | | |
| **Fireplace** | | | | |
| Damper | | | | |
| Chimney and flue | | | | |
| Mortar joints | | | | |
| Flashings | | | | |
| Ash collector | | | | |

| Interior | Dates Checked | | | Remarks |
|---|---|---|---|---|
| **Heating and Air-Conditioning (HVAC)** | | | | |
| Humidifier | | | | |
| Filters | | | | |
| Air registers and returns | | | | |
| Ducts and dampers | | | | |
| Thermostat | | | | |
| Blower fan* | | | | |
| Burners* | | | | |
| Motor* | | | | |
| Pilot* | | | | |
| Flue and chimney* | | | | |
| Gas line* | | | | |
| Refrigerant* | | | | |
| **Interior Surfaces (Check for cleaning, refinishing, and repairing)** | | | | |
| Ceilings | | | | |
| Walls | | | | |
| Floors | | | | |
| Trim and molding | | | | |

*May be part of an annual professional inspection.

| Interior | Dates Checked | | | Remarks |
|---|---|---|---|---|
| **Plumbing** | | | | |
| Faucets | | | | |
| Pipe connections | | | | |
| Drains | | | | |
| Aerators | | | | |
| **Water Heater** | | | | |
| Pressure relief valve | | | | |
| Mineral deposits | | | | |
| Temperature setting | | | | |
| **Windows and Doors** | | | | |
| Caulking | | | | |
| Sashes | | | | |
| Thresholds | | | | |
| Hinges, handles, locks | | | | |
| Painted surfaces | | | | |
| Tracks and rollers | | | | |
| Weatherstripping | | | | |

| Exterior | Dates Checked | | | Remarks |
|---|---|---|---|---|
| **Exterior Surfaces (Check for cleaning, refinishing, and repairing)** | | | | |
| Masonry | | | | |
| Siding | | | | |
| Trim and Molding | | | | |
| **Foundation** | | | | |
| Masonry joints and surfaces (Check for cracks and termites) | | | | |
| **Drainage** | | | | |
| Check foundations of deck, porches, and patio | | | | |
| **Grounds and Miscellaneous** | | | | |
| Driveway | | | | |
| Sidewalks and steps | | | | |
| Lawn | | | | |
| Trees, shrubs, and other plant | | | | |
| Grades (Slope of the ground) | | | | |
| Drains and splash blocks | | | | |
| Walls, fences, gates | | | | |
| Recreation equipment | | | | |
| Exterior lights and outlets | | | | |
| Septic tank | | | | |
| Address identification | | | | |

| Exterior | Dates Checked | | | Remarks |
|---|---|---|---|---|
| **Grounds and Miscellaneous (Continued)** | | | | |
| Mailbox | | | | |
| Utility entrances and meters | | | | |
| **Roof** | | | | |
| Roofing | | | | |
| Chimney | | | | |
| Flashing | | | | |
| Vents | | | | |
| Antenna mounts | | | | |
| Gutters and downspouts | | | | |
| **Windows and Doors** | | | | |
| Caulking | | | | |
| Glazing | | | | |
| Screens | | | | |
| Storm windows and doors | | | | |
| Shutters | | | | |
| Skylights | | | | |
| Weatherstripping | | | | |

# Suppliers and Contractors

Store this booklet with all the instruction manuals and manufacturers' warranties you receive with your new home in a convenient place, so the information is easy to find when you need it.

| Item | Name | Phone |
|---|---|---|
| Air-conditioning | | |
| Brickwork | | |
| Cabinetwork | | |
| Ceramic tile | | |
| Concrete or cement | | |
| Countertop | | |
| Dishwasher | | |
| Disposal | | |
| Driveway | | |
| Drywall | | |
| Electrician | | |
| Fireplace | | |
| Garage doors | | |
| Gutters and downspouts | | |
| HVAC system | | |
| Insulation | | |
| Landscaping | | |
| Masonry | | |
| Microwave oven | | |

| Item | Name | Phone |
|---|---|---|
| Millwork (doors, windows, trim, etc.) | | |
| Painting | | |
| Plaster | | |
| Plumbing and fixtures | | |
| Range, oven, broiler | | |
| Refrigerator | | |
| Resilient flooring | | |
| Roofing | | |
| Security system | | |
| Siding | | |
| Sliding glass doors | | |
| Trash compactor | | |
| Washer and dryer | | |
| Water heater | | |
| Weatherstripping | | |
| Wood flooring | | |

# Warranty Notes

| Item | Serial # | Model | Warranty | Service Provider |
|---|---|---|---|---|
| **Appliances** | | | | |
| Clothes dryer | | | | |
| Clothes washer | | | | |
| Dishwasher | | | | |
| Freezer | | | | |
| Garbage disposal | | | | |
| Ice maker | | | | |
| Microwave | | | | |
| Oven and hood | | | | |
| Refrigerator | | | | |
| Range, stove, or cooktop | | | | |
| Trash compactor | | | | |

**HVAC System**

| | | | | |
|---|---|---|---|---|
| Air conditioning | | | | |
| Boiler | | | | |
| Electronic air cleaner | | | | |
| Exhaust fan | | | | |
| Furnace | | | | |
| Heat pump | | | | |
| Humidifier | | | | |
| Space heater | | | | |
| Thermostat | | | | |

| Item | Serial # | Model | Warranty | Service Provider |
|---|---|---|---|---|
| **Mechanical and/or Electrical** | | | | |
| Burglar alarm | | | | |
| Carbon monoxide detector | | | | |
| Central vacuum system | | | | |
| Doorbell | | | | |
| Electric meter | | | | |
| Fire alarm | | | | |
| Fire extinguisher | | | | |
| Garage door opener | | | | |
| Gas meter | | | | |
| Gas or electric barbecue grill | | | | |
| Intercom | | | | |
| Radon detector | | | | |
| Smoke detector | | | | |
| Water meter | | | | |
| Water pump | | | | |

**Plumbing**

| | | | | |
|---|---|---|---|---|
| Sump pump | | | | |
| Water heater | | | | |
| Water softener | | | | |

# Notes